Dinosaur Facts for Kids

Jacquelyn Elnor Johnson

www.CrimsonHillBooks.com

First edition, May 2022.

Cataloguing in Publication Data

Johnson, Jacquelyn Elnor

Dinosaur Facts for Kids

Description: Crimson Hill Books trade paperback edition | Nova Scotia, Canada

ISBN:	978-1-990887-09-3 (Paperback - Ingram)
BISAC:	JNF003050 Juvenile Nonfiction: Animals - Dinosaurs & Prehistoric Creatures JNF025150 Juvenile Nonfiction: History - Prehistoric JNF037050 Juvenile Nonfiction: Science & Nature - Fossils
THEMA:	RBX - Paleontology WNA - Dinosaurs & the prehistoric world - general interest YNNA - Children's - Teenage general interest - Dinosaurs & prehistoric world

Record available at https://www.bac-lac.gc.ca/eng/Pages/home.aspx

Book design: Jesse Johnson

Crimson Hill Books
(a division of)
Crimson Hill Products Inc.
Lawrencetown, Nova Scotia
Canada

Crimson Hill
Books

A pack of Tyrannosaurus rex fighting an Ankylosaurus.

Tyrannosaurus rex is the world's most famous dinosaur, but it wasn't the largest or the fastest or even the strangest dinosaur that ever lived. There are many more fantastic and fascinating dinosaurs to discover!

Do you know dinosaurs?

For many thousands of years, storytellers told myths and legends about strange and monstrous creatures. These creatures were called dragons. There were many fantastical things about dragons. They were huge, but they could fly. They were very strong, but not very smart. Their job was guarding princesses from all sorts of trouble. And, most incredible of all, they could breathe out great plumes of fire. Dragons were fierce, dangerous and fascinating!

Yet there was no proof that they ever existed. Perhaps dragons were just creatures of the imagination, like characters in a video game or movie or on TV. They were big, bad and fun to think about and tell stories about, but dragons weren't real.

People all over the world enjoyed these dragon stories for many thousands of years. At the same time, many people said that nothing like a dragon had ever existed and could never exist. They were too different from animals that are alive today to ever be real. Many people in the past believed all the types of animals that have ever lived were still alive now. Animals don't change, they argued. The Earth and everything on it including all the plants and animals, and humans, too, have always been exactly the same.

No one had proof about how old the Earth might be. They didn't know how Earth started or when. They didn't know when plants, animals and people got here. The dragon question was just one thing that scientists, and everyone else, wondered about. This caused a lot of arguments about these questions and a lot of crazy ideas to try to answer them.

Ichthyovenator [Ick-fee-oh-ven-a-tor] was a spinosaurid dinosaur that lived in Laos, Asia in the early Cretaceous Era. Spinosaurids were the dinosaurs with spines and possibly sails on their backs.

Then, only about 200 years ago, some bones and fossils were found that didn't seem to match any known living creature. Scientists couldn't figure out just what they were but gave this question creature a name anyways. That name is dinosaur. It means "giant lizard."

Dinosaurs aren't giant lizards, but the name stuck. They also weren't dragons (though there were some people who still wished they were). As scientists studied these bones and fossils, they realized that dinosaurs couldn't fly. Some of them were huge, but some weren't. Maybe the smaller ones were the babies of the bigger ones? Or maybe they were a different animal? They just didn't know.

Gargoyleosaurus [Gar-goi-el-lee-oh-sore-us] was a slow-moving armored tank of an animal that ate plants and lived in the late Jurassic Period.

The biggest ones were bigger than a school bus. The smallest ones could have fit in a cat-carrier. One thing they did know is no animal including dinosaurs ever had a furnace in its belly. They couldn't breathe fire.

Today, scientists have much better tools to discover what dinosaurs really were and how they lived. They can use x-rays and body scans to get a look at the inside of dinosaurs' skulls to study how their brains and ears worked. They can use computer animation software to study how these animals walked and ran. They look through high-powered microscopes at dinosaurs' skin and feathers. Scientists of the past didn't have these detection tools.

All the dinosaurs lived on land. They were all either plant-eaters or meat-eaters. They were probably reptiles, but we're still not sure about this because in some ways they were very different than all the reptiles that are alive today.

Dinosaurs weren't lizards, though as far as we know they were probably all reptiles or at least reptile-like. They weren't all huge, like dragons. Dinosaurs came in all sizes, from the size of a modern chicken to some that were bigger than a fire truck.

We can't know Dinosaurs the way we know horses, or dogs, or any other animal alive today. The reason is no human has ever seen a living dinosaur. They appeared on Earth and were here for millions of years. Then, suddenly, all the dinosaurs were gone. They all became extinct, long before humans arrived on Earth.

There is no zoo or animal park where you could go to see dinosaurs that are alive. Their time on Earth ended long before human time began.

Every year, paleontologists [say this: pay-lee-on-tall-oh-jists] are discovering more of these amazing animals and more about the ones that are already named. Paleontologists are the scientists who study ancient animals, including dinosaurs. At last, the creatures who were hidden for so long are revealing some of their strange secrets.

Today, scientists have named and described more than 1,550 different species of dinosaurs. There are probably many more we haven't found yet. It could be, over all those millions of years, there were thousands more dinosaurs that are still hidden in ancient rocks, just waiting to be discovered. Here are the facts we know so far about the largest, fiercest, strangest animals that have ever lived.

What is a dinosaur?

Dinosaurs were one large and very diverse family of animals. Diverse means there were lots of differences in the dino family. They came in all shapes and sizes. Some had feathers; others had fur. Some could run fast, but others could only walk slowly. Some could swim, though none of them lived in water. There were also some that could glide between the trees and might have been able to fly.

Their ancestor was another animal group called Archosaurs. Archosaurs are also the ancestor of all crocodiles and birds.

Dinosaurs were a group of animals that seem almost as fantastical as dragons. They were magnificent animals and they were real. Dinosaurs thrived for more than 165 million years.

Some dinosaurs had horns or feathers sticking out of their faces. Others had large horns or spiny sails on their backs or body armor. Some walked on their hind legs while others walked on all four feet. There were dinosaurs that had knife-sharp teeth. Some had beaks, but no teeth. Most of them had tails.

Unlike almost all reptiles today, dinosaurs had a special advantage. Their legs were under their bodies, not coming out of the sides of their bodies like modern reptiles. They were different from other reptiles because they had a pelvis that allowed them to walk upright on two legs. They had extra vertebrae, or back bones. Some dinosaurs also had strong arms.

Over millions of years, they changed to became stronger and larger, until they lived everywhere on Earth. They weren't the only animals on Earth in their time, but for millions of years, they were the top animals everywhere except in the oceans.

Were dinosaurs cold-blooded?

Every animal alive today, including humans, is either cold-blooded or warm-blooded. This doesn't mean the actual temperature of their blood. It means how their body works.

Cold-blooded animals can't control their own body temperatures. They don't have ways to cool off or warm up when they need to. A cold-blooded animal has to find a shady place when it gets too warm, or a warm spot when it gets too cold. This sounds like a bad thing, but it isn't. That's because cold-blooded animals don't have to eat as much food. They can go a long time with no food at all. They don't need energy from food to warm up or cool off. This helps them survive.

Warm-blooded animals have to eat more food more often. All birds and mammals including people are warm-blooded. We use food energy to warm our bodies. We can also shiver to warm up or sweat to cool down. No reptile, and also as far as we know no dinosaur, can or ever could do this.

Lambeosaurus [Lam-bee-oh-sore-us] was a Hadrosaur that lived in North America during the Cretaceous Era.

For now, most scientists believe that the dinosaurs were all reptiles. Not everyone is sure about this. But what if some dinosaurs weren't cold-blooded or warm-blooded? What if dinosaurs were something else? Some experts think that some dinosaurs might have been not cold-blooded, or warm-blooded, but a mix of these two.

If so, then they were dinosaur-blooded. What would such an animal be like? There's no animal like this on Earth today. It's an intriguing idea, but there is no proof yet that all dinosaurs were cold-blooded reptiles like the reptiles we know now.

The three types of dinosaurs

Dinosaurs started off as small, quick animals and evolved into three main types. Evolved means their kind changed very slowly, over many millions of years.

Ornithischian [or-nith-itch-chee-an] dinosaurs had leaf-shaped teeth. They were all the dinosaurs with strange faces like the plant-eaters with beaks, the ones with a duck bill called Hadrosaurs and the dinosaurs that had spikes or horns. Some walked on their back two legs, while others walked on all-four legs. All Ornithischian dinosaurs had bird-hips. They're called this because the bones of their hips are the same shape as modern birds, even though they aren't the ancestors of birds.

Hadrosaurs traveled in herds. They migrated, like some modern birds. These duck-billed dinosaurs were preyed upon by carnivores, or meat-eaters. They laid their eggs near rivers once a year and always returned to the same nesting place.

Sauropods [saw-ruh-pods] were the long-necks with pot bellies and tiny heads. They are the largest land animals that have ever lived. Titanosaurs are in this group. Sauropods had reptile-shaped hips, just like modern lizards and crocodiles do. They had air sacs attached to their lungs and hollow bones. This worked like an air-conditioning system inside their bodies.

Theropods [theh-ruh-pods] were the meat-eating dinosaurs, including Tyrannosaurs like T-rex. They also had reptile hips. Strangely, all modern birds, who do have bird-hips, evolved from some of the smaller

Theropods. Theropods were the top hunter-predators during their time. They're also the most diverse looking group among the three types of dinosaurs. A very small group of Theropods were omnivores. This means they ate both plants and meat.

When was the first dinosaur discovered?

For a long time, probably thousands of years, people had found strange bones and rock formations and footprints. They had no idea what these could be from. Monsters, maybe. Or dragons. Or even possibly visitors from outer space. There were lots of stories.

It wasn't until two hundred years ago, in 1824 in England, that a scientist looked at some of the strange things that had been found and said all these stories were ridiculous. William Buckland took a close look at some fossils and said they couldn't be dragons. The bones didn't match any known animal, either. This meant that the remains had to be a mysterious new kind of animal. In fact, a newly discovered, very ancient animal.

Mr. Buckland thought this animal was probably a giant reptile. Lots of people laughed at this idea. Others were just very confused. There was one expert who insisted that the bones came from an ancient race of giant humans, possibly people like Goliath in The Bible.

What if these fossils weren't animals at all, some people asked. It could be just very old wood. Or

This is a Velociraptor [Vell-oh-seer-rap-tor] skeleton that has turned into a fossil. Velociraptor was a late Cretaceous Era Theropod.

strange rocks. There could be no such thing as an animal people didn't already know about, many people believed. Others thought Mr. Buckland just might be right. It would take many more years of study, by many scientists, to understand just what these fossils were.

In 1842, scientist Richard Owen made a major breakthrough. He looked at all the fossil bones and realized they didn't belong to just one animal. The fossils had to come from a group of animals, he said. In time, with more study, more experts decided he must be right.

This is the fossil of a small reptile that lived millions of years ago. With five clawed fingers and toes, it looks very much like a lizard that lives today.

Megalosaurus [Meg-ga-low-sore-us] was the first dinosaur to get its own name. It was a Theropod. It had a large head and walked on two strong legs. It had smaller arms and three fingers with claws. It also had sharp, curved teeth to rip at other dinosaurs, reptiles, and small animals it ate. Megalosaurus used its long tail for balance. This meant it could walk or run.

Megalsaurus lived 166 million years ago, in the Jurassic period. Its fossils have only ever been found near the city of Oxford in England.

How do we know about dinosaurs?

Paleontologists, or palaeontologists, are the scientists who study fossils to learn about the history of life on Earth. This includes the history of animals like dinosaurs. They work like detectives, investigating all the evidence that the plants and animals of long ago left behind. They find clues in rocks and the fossils that are in the rocks, in ancient footprints or trackways frozen in stone, and sometimes in other places, like small creatures or parts of their bodies in amber.

Trackways are a line of footprints that show where the animal was going. Amber is ancient tree sap that has hardened into an orange stone. You might have seen amber that is made into jewellery. When you look very closely, you might see a tiny bug or leaf locked in the amber. Dinosaurs were too big to be trapped in amber. They are more likely to be fossils.

Almost everything we know about the dinosaurs is based on fossils of their bones, teeth, skin prints, claws and eggs.

One famous paleontologist was Barnum Brown, an American who is remembered as a great dinosaur hunter. He began his career at the American Museum of Natural History in New York City in 1897. He studied the first remains of a Tyrannosaurus rex found in Montana. It was an almost-complete skeleton, a very rare find. Usually, bones and fossils are all mixed up when a group of animals died at the same time, perhaps in a mudslide, during a sudden flood or by getting trapped in quicksand. The T-rex Mr. Brown studied is still on display in the Museum's dinosaur hall, where you can see it today if you visit New York.

Usually, paleontologists have only a very small part of an animal to use as they try to understand what an animal looked like and how it lived. They might only have one vertebra to study. Vertebrae (that means more than one) are the bones that together make up an animal's spine, or backbone. All reptiles, birds, amphibians, fish and mammals have a spine.

With so little evidence to work with, paleontologists can make mistakes. One famous paleontologist, Gideon Mantell, who lived from 1790 to 1852, put Iguanodon's thumb claw on top of its nose. His model of Iguanodon stayed that way, thumbing its nose, for the next 40 years.

Edward Cope also made a funny mistake when he put together a skeleton of Elasmosaurus. It had its head on the end of its tail. Until not long ago, museums displayed Apatosaurus with the wrong name, calling it

The fossil vertebrae of this dinosaur are the bones at the top of its back. In life, bones are pink, not black. They turned black when the bones turned to stone.

Brontosaurus. And they put a Camarasaurus head on the Apatosaurus body. It took a while for scientists to realize this was totally wrong, and even longer for museum officials to agree and fix their exhibits.

For decades, paleontologists thought large dinos were so big that they must have needed two brains. Otherwise, they said, it would just take too long for a message from their tail to get all the way up to the brain in their head. They must have had two brains, they decided. One up in their head, and one closer to their behind. Today, it sounds ridiculous. But people really thought this, a hundred years ago or so.

What is a fossil?

After an animal dies, their bones slowly decompose on or in the ground. This means they break down, rot away and are gone. Very rarely, before this happens, bones can turn into stone. This is called fossilization or fossilisation.

Bones, teeth, claws, or eggs can be fossilized. Nearly all the fossils scientists and amateur fossil-hunters have found are from animals that lived in rivers, lakes, or oceans. This means paleontologists have a lot more fossils from fish, clams, sharks, and other sea creatures than from land animals like dinosaurs.

Here's how some parts of an animal can turn into fossils.

1. The animal dies.
2. The soft parts of the animal are eaten by other animals or they rot away, leaving just the hard parts, like bones, spines, teeth, claws or horns.
3. These hard body parts are covered and buried by mud, sand, or silt.
4. More sand or silt or mud lands on top of them. This puts weight and pressure on the buried body.
5. Water and minerals move into the bones or other hard body pieces, gradually turning to stone. All of the real body parts are gone. Only the stone remains.

We don't really know exactly how long this whole process takes, but it could be millions of years. The reason most fossils that fossil-hunters find are from marine animals is because an animal that lives in water will sink to the bottom and could quickly be covered by silt or sand. Land animals, like dinosaurs, did need to live close to water. Some of them would have died because they were caught in quicksand or buried by a mudslide.

Paleontologists are able to find some dino fossils because the Earth is always building itself up and tearing itself down at the same time. Rock layers are pushed up to the surface and mountains are created. These layers are also always getting worn down by the weather and erosion. Wind, ice, rain, heat, and rivers cutting through mountains can cause fossils to move closer to the surface.

The other main reason fossils are found is just good luck. It might be that a sharp-eyed person spots something odd sticking out of the ground. They think it might be a horse skeleton, or maybe just a piece of wood. They call the local university, or maybe the local heritage office and, sometimes, what they've found is something really remarkable, like a part of the jawbone or spine of a dinosaur!

Two types of fossils

Paleontologists look for body fossils and trace fossils.

Body fossils are any part of a plant or animal. They could be leaves, bones, horns, quills, feathers or teeth.

Trace fossils are evidence of an animal's behaviour. Some trace fossils are hand prints, foot prints, burrows, bite marks, eggs, nests or tail drag marks.

Where did dinosaurs come from and when?

Dinosaurs were not the first animals on Earth. There were plenty of animals here already when they arrived. All the dinosaurs lived during the Mesozoic Era of history. It started 252 million years ago and ended 65 ½ or 66 million years ago.

The very first dinosaurs were small and could run fast. They could easily catch the other small or baby animals they ate. Very gradually, their bodies changed to give them even more advantages to survive. Advantages are useful things to have, like better hearing or eyesight, or stronger muscles, or hunting skills.

Over their very long time on Earth, dinosaurs became bigger, stronger and more diverse. Diverse means there were lots of differences. It happens because Nature is always experimenting with what might work better in a plant or an animal. Would it be better to have five eyes, like some insects do, or just two? Would feathers be better than scales? Or fur? Or just bare skin? And what about claws? Or should this creature have hooves instead? Or maybe learn to fly?

Dinosaur Fun Fact:

Most dinosaur fossils have been found in United States, Canada, Argentina, China and, recently, Antarctica. If you plan on doing some fossil hunting, these are all good places to look!

Though it looked like a dinosaur, Dimetrodon [Di-met-tro-don] was a reptile, but not a dinosaur. It became extinct about 60 million years before dinosaurs evolved.

Very gradually, animals and plants change. This kind of change is called "evolving." The science of how evolving works is called "evolution." It happens to give all living things an advantage, or several advantages, to suit where they live. The creatures with the best advantages are the ones who are most likely to live long enough to have babies. This way, they pass their advantages along to the next generation.

What is evolution?

Evolution [ev-oh-loo-shun] is how animals make tiny changes over time. Every living thing has evolved on Earth since it was created. Every living thing continues to evolve, as they all will until the end of time.

You could say that evolution started 4.5 billion years ago, when another planet, called Theia, crashed into Earth. One small chunk broke off and became our moon. Much later, our oceans formed, and that is where the first life began with tiny animals. Each one had only one cell.

Millions of years passed. Some cells came together and became very small creatures. More time passed as these small creatures became larger ones, like jelly fish, and later, fish.

Some fish got larger and fiercer, like sharks. Some eventually left the oceans and moved onto land. Their fins made many small changes to finally became legs with feet. Over millions of years, some fish evolved into Tetrapods. Later still, some Tetrapods became Amphibians. Some Amphibians gradually became Reptiles.

One type of reptile evolved into dinosaurs about two hundred million years ago. Another type of reptile, the Therapsids, very slowly evolved into Mammals. Eventually, one Mammal evolved into humans. There were many types of humans, but only our own type, named Homo Sapiens, is alive today.

Permian Era

299 million years ago to 252 million years ago

This was the long period of time that came before the age of dinosaurs. In this time, Earth had only one huge continent, called Pangea. There was only one vast ocean. Pangea was a hot, dry place. Most of it was a desert. Animals lived in or next to the lakes, rivers and the ocean. The temperature on some days near the Equator might have been as hot as 74º Celsius or 165º Fahrenheit. The dominant animals, that means the ones that ruled, in the Permian Era were all Therapsids, our ancient ancestors. All the reptiles were small.

In the Permian Era, all the plants were ferns or conifers or small shrubs. Conifers are evergreen trees. There were sharks, bony fish, insects, worms and millipedes. There were giant salamanders and crocodiles. There were also reptiles. The first true mammals would not appear until the next geological period, the Triassic.

Periods in time tend to end with an extinction event. This means something terrible happens and a lot of plants and animals die. The Permian Era became hotter and drier. Drought became more common.

There was more competition for water and food. Volcanos erupted, making the world drier, hotter, and darkening the skies.

The Permian ended with The Great Dying when massive volcanos released gasses into the air that caused Earth to get too hot for many animals to survive. Some reptiles, crocodiles, fish, ocean animals, amphibians like frogs and insects did survive. Extinction events always leave room for new types of animals to develop in the next era. One would be the dinosaurs, a new type of reptile.

Mesozoic Era

252 million years ago to 65.5 million years ago

The Mesozoic Era followed the Permian Era. The skies cleared of ash and the rains came. Pangea cooled but still had a tropical climate. It was warmer than most of the world is today. There was also more oxygen in the air than there is now. Animals that could live in this warm, wet world survived.

For all of the long Mesozoic Era, the weather was warm and tropical, everywhere in the world. The climate would have gotten a bit cooler at times, or a bit warmer, but there never was an Ice Age.

The Mesozoic Era is divided into three separate periods of early, middle years and later. These three are called the Triassic, Jurassic and Cretaceous. Each one ended, and brought in the next one, with a smaller extinction event, when some animals and plants became extinct while others survived.

Placodus

Arizonasaurus

Batrachotomus

Coelophysis

Cymbospondylus

Mastodonsaurus

Arizonasaurus

Batrachotomus

Peteinosaurus

Desmatosuchus

Triassic
Dinosaurs

Lystrosaurus

Proganochelys Turtle

Prestosuchus

Plateosaurus

Nothosaurus

Hupehsuchus

Triassic Era

252 million years ago to 201 million years ago

As the Triassic began, there were still inland deserts in Pangea. There were insects and worms, but no snakes yet. In the oceans, there were sharks and giant marine reptiles. On land in this warm world there were ferns the size of trees, and also conifers and ginkgo trees.

Insects continued to evolve and the first grasshoppers appeared. During the Mesozoic Era, Pangea would split into two continents and then into the continents we know today. In some parts of Pangea, a new type of reptile evolved. In what is now Scotland 245 million years ago, one early dinosaur called Saltopus lived. There were also early dinosaurs in what became South America, and probably other places, although they haven't been found yet.

The earliest dinosaurs were carnivores, the name for meat-eaters. Or some could have been omnivores, the name for animals that eat plants and meat. Later on, herbivore dinosaurs appeared. Herbivore means they only eat plants.

In the Triassic Era, the dominant animal was Pseudosuchias [Sue-doe-sooch-ee-as], a pre-crocodile. For the first 20 million years that there were dinosaurs, Earth was ruled by prehistoric crocodiles.

Dinosaur Fun Fact:
Some dinosaurs could retract their claws, like cats do.

The Triassic Era ended with an extinction event when half of all the animals died out, but most reptiles, mammals and dinosaurs survived. In the next era, the mammals would remain small, but the dinosaurs became bigger, more powerful, and then they dominated the world.

Jurassic Era

201 million years ago to 145.5 million years ago

In the Jurassic, Pangea got a bit cooler than it was during the Permian Era, though it was still warmer than almost everywhere on Earth is today. Temperatures were in the middle 30 degrees Celsius, or in the middle 80 degrees Fahrenheit, a lot like a hot summer day is in the modern world. Now, there was more rain. While the forests became bigger, the deserts shrank. New rivers and lakes formed. With lots of sun and rain there was plenty for the plant-eaters to eat. That mean there were lots of plant-eaters for the meat-eaters to eat. Dinosaurs got larger and stronger in this era. They thrived.

Early in this period, Pangea split in two. One half, called Laurasia, drifted north. The other half, Gondwana, drifted south.

In the middle of the Jurassic, about 178 million years ago, the first true mammals appeared. Mammals were different from reptiles because their babies were born alive, not in an egg like most reptiles and fish. Other ways mammals were different are they fed their babies with milk, were warm-blooded and had fur.

Dilophosaurus

Apatosaurus

Dicraeosaurus

Allosaurus

Spinophosaurus

Kentosaurus

Atlasaurus

Archaeopteryx

Diplodocus

Jurassic
Dinosaurs

Stegosaurus

Compsognathus

Brachiosaurus

Ornitholestes

Ceratosaurus

Cryolophosaurus

Dorygnathus

All early mammals lived underground in burrows. They were mostly active at night because that was the safest time to be out and about. There were fewer reptiles and dinosaurs awake at night to hunt them.

The largest early mammal was Repenomamus [Re-pen-oh-ma-mus]. It looked something like a modern opossum or badger. It ate dinosaur eggs and small dinosaurs as well as other small reptiles like lizards. In the Mesozoic Era, mammals never got bigger than weighing 50 pounds, or 23 kilograms. Most of them were much smaller, more like modern rodents. Rodents of today are rats, mice, squirrels, and chipmunks. Rodents are the largest group among mammals alive today.

Climate change and rising sea levels ended the Jurassic Era. Most of the Stegosaurs and the long-neck dinosaurs died out. Stegosaurs were the armoured dinosaurs that walked on four legs, like Ankylosaurus [Ann-kill-oh-sore-us].

Cretaceous Era

145.5 million years ago to 66 million years ago

During the Cretaceous Era, the sea levels rose and fell many times. The two continents split apart into the ones we know today and began to drift across the oceans to where they are now.

Dinosaurs, and all the other plants and land animals, travelled on these drifting continents. With no land bridges, the dinosaurs became more diverse. Though

Cretaceous Dinosaurs

Parasaurolophus

Styracosaurus

Amargasaurus

Pentaceratops

Pachycephalosaurus

Utahraptor

Olorotitan

Diabloceratops

Carnotaurus

Tenontosaurus

Antarctosaurus

Kaprosuchus

Nanotyrannus

Velociraptor

Torosaurus

Tyrannosaurus Rex

Deinonychus

the ones in Asia were something like the ones in North America or Australia or Africa, they also evolved to survive better where they lived.

At this time, Europe was many islands separated by shallow, warm seas. Thick layers of sand and mud built up at the bottom of these seas as small creatures died and their skeletons fell to the seabed. This is how chalk was first formed. The word "Cretaceous" comes from the Latin word that means "chalk."

The Cretaceous Era is when the first flowers and the first grasses appeared. Trees changed, too. Willow, elm, laurel, birch, oak, and maple trees evolved, and so did the sequoia trees of California. In the skies there were the first birds.

In North America, the Rocky Mountains rose. The centre of that continent, where the Great American Plains and Canadian Prairies are today, was an inland ocean. Many of the North American dinosaurs we know of today lived on its shores.

This was the Age of the Dinosaurs, when they became the largest land animals that have ever lived. There were herds of duck-billed Hadrosaurs. Packs of hunting Titanosaurs. It was also the time of the giant crocodiles.

Dinosaur Fun Fact:

There is one animal alive today that is the closest known relative of Tyrannosaurus rex. It's a creature you probably eat sometimes. What is it? The chicken!

Everything was bigger, fiercer, and probably louder than ever before, except for the mammals. They still hid in their burrows, or scurried outside. It would be in a future era that their time would finally come.

Were all dinosaurs reptiles?

All dinosaurs were reptiles or reptile-like animals. They built nests and laid eggs, just like modern reptiles do. The one difference dinosaurs had from reptiles is their legs were under their bodies, like mammals. Almost all modern reptiles except birds have legs that are attached to the sides of their bodies.

What colors were dinosaurs?

Modern animals use color to hide, like camo clothing. Or to impress others, like people use really cool clothes. Or to attract a mate.

Some animals can change color, like chameleons or some lizards, depending on if they are too hot, or too cold. Or to blend in with their home and not be seen by their enemies.

We also know that in tropical countries, animals tend to have brighter colors. In cooler countries, closer to the North Pole or the South Pole, animals tend to be mostly darker or duller colors like black, brown, or gray. Not all animals, but most of them use color as a survival tool. They have adapted with whatever gives them the best chance to survive.

Artists can only imagine what colors dinosaurs really were. All we have left of the dinosaurs are just their footprints, fossils and bones and these can't tell us what colors they were.

Scientists have long thought that dinosaurs probably used their colors just like modern animals do. Now, with more powerful microscopes, they are able to look at traces of pigment left in dinosaur feathers. They've discovered that dinosaurs were as colorful as modern animals. Dinosaurs were black, brown, gray or white with some red. Some had stripes of bands of color. Others were camo colors.

Dinosaur Fun Fact:

Dinosaurs ruled Earth for over 150 million years.

Einiosaurus [Een-ee-oh-sore-us] was a Ceratopsian dinosaur, like Triceratops. It was a herbivore and lived 74 million years ago in Montana, United States. The Ceratopsians were the dinos with bony frills and beak bones.

Dinosaur Fun Fact:

Every year, paleontologists and amateur fossil hunters discover another 50 types of dinosaurs. That's almost one new dinosaur every week!

What did dinosaurs eat?

There are three types of eaters, in dinosaur times and today. They are:

Herbivores – They only eat plants or things that come from plants like bark, roots, fruit or seeds. Plant-eating animals usually live in herds for protection. Horses, sheep and goats are modern herbivores.

Carnivores – They only eat meat from other animals. Dinosaurs that were carnivores ate young or injured animals. They sometimes ate their own kind including their own babies. Carnivores usually live and hunt either alone or in small packs. All types of cats and raptors are carnivores.

Omnivores – They eat both plant products and meat. Bears, dogs, some insects and most people are omnivores.

Paleontologists find out about what dinosaurs ate by studying their teeth, or fossils of their teeth. The herbivores, or plant-eaters, had smaller teeth but more of them, because they wore out their teeth quickly chewing on bark and twigs as well as leaves. They must have had new teeth growing in all the time.

The meat-eaters, or carnivores, also had lots of teeth but they were larger, sharper and stronger. These teeth were used to rip meat from the body of any animal they killed or found already dead.

About one third of all dinosaurs were carnivores and the other two-thirds were herbivores. Very few were omnivores. That's also true of animals alive today.

Were dinosaurs smart?

Dinosaurs were big but dumb. That's what a lot of people used to think about them or any animal that seemed to have a small brain compared to how big its body was.

But is this really true? Dinosaurs had to be smart enough to do what every animal needs to be able to do. This is find fresh water, healthy food, shelter and mates. They had to be smart enough to survive, which they did, for a very long time.

Today, scientists agree that dinos were probably about as smart as modern animals. Maybe they were smarter than that. All we have is their fossils, bones and footprints. That's not enough to know nearly as much as we'd like to know about them.

So, what are the smartest dinosaur species that could outsmart prey? The smartest dinosaurs were possibly the Troodontids [True-doon-tids], paleontologists say. Troodontids were a group of bird-like dinosaurs that had a large brain compared to how big their bodies were. Their brain was closer to most birds of today, not like an average reptile brain. Other smart hunter predators are Compsognathus (it was also bird-like), Dromaeosaurids (including Velociraptor), and Tyrannosaurs and the close T-rex cousins Spinosaurus, Allosaurus, and Giganotosaurus.

Dinosaur Fun Fact:
The fearsome Allosaurus, the top predator in the Jurassic Era, went extinct in the Cretaceous Era. Scientists don't know why.

Microraptors were small, four-winged dinosaurs with feathers. They lived in China. They could glide and might have been able to fly.

Were all dinosaurs huge?

Dinosaurs came in all sizes. The earlier ones were all smaller. Later on, they got bigger. Today, the largest ones are the most popular with kids. It's true that we don't find very many dinosaur fossils, compared to fossils from other animals. The dino fossils that are discovered are almost always from the larger dinosaurs, who had bigger claws, horns, teeth or bones. Smaller animals, with smaller bones, were less likely to become fossils.

Were there mammoths when the dinosaurs lived?

There weren't any wooly mammoths roaming Earth in the Age of Dinosaurs. Mammoths, giant sloths and Sabre cats lived in the Pleistocene Era. That was 63 million years after the end of the Mesozoic Era, when all the dinosaurs became extinct.

Why did some dinosaurs have feathers?

Dinosaurs didn't all have smooth skin like most modern lizards. Instead, some had scales or plates, like body armor, to protect them. Others had feathers. But why would they have feathers when they couldn't fly?

Some paleontologists think the feathers were for keeping warm. They say the feathers are evidence that these types of dinosaurs were warm-blooded, like birds and mammals today. Feathers may also have been for attracting a mate, or just for show.

Who was the smallest dinosaur?

We don't know for sure who was the very smallest dinosaur. They might not have been found yet. But here are some little guys that might be in the Smallest Dino Contest.

Anchiornis [An-chee-or-nes] was about as big as a pigeon, with long legs and wings. It was covered in feathers. It could probably glide, but we don't know if it was strong enough to flap its wings and fly. It looked something like a modern falcon, but with a chicken's head. It was about 13 inches to 16 inches long, or 34 centimetres to 40 centimeters long.

This is one of very few dinosaurs that we do know what color they were. This is because some pigment cells were still in their fossils, found in China. Pigment is what gives skin or hair, or feathers, their colors. Anchiornis was mainly dark gray and black, with a red crown and white stripes on its wings.

Epidexipteryx [Epp-i-dex-ip-ter-icks] was another small dinosaur a bit like a bird. It lived in Asia around 160 to 168 million years ago, in the mid to late Jurassic period. It had four long tail feathers and might have been a glider, climbing up trees and then gliding between them until it reached the ground.

Parvicursor [Par-vee-cur-sore], had long, thin legs. It lived in what is now Mongolia during the late Cretaceous period. It was only 39 centimetres, or 15 inches long.

Aquilops [Ak-kwill-ops] was a tiny horned and frilled dinosaur that lived in North America. It weighed just 3 pounds, or 1.3 kilograms and lived 110 million years ago. It was tiny, for a dinosaur, but was the ancestor of later and very much larger plant-eaters including Triceratops and Styracosaurus.

Dinosaur Fun Fact:
An adult T-rex needed to eat 200 pounds or 91 kilograms of meat every day.

Compsognathus was a small, fast hunter that ate lizards and small mammals.

Compsognathus [Comp-sog-nay-thus] was about 39 inches, or 1 metre long and weighed just 6.5 pounds, or 2.5 kilograms. It lived in Europe from 151 million years ago to 140 million years ago.

Its fossils have been found in Germany, France, and Portugal.

What do dinosaur footprints tell us?

You might think that you can't tell much from just a footprint, but you'd be wrong about that. From just one footprint, paleontologists and other scientists can know how tall the animal that made that footprint was and about how much it weighed. If you measure a footprint, and multiply that number by 4, you know how long their leg bone was.

A footprint can also tell you what type of dinosaur made it. A print with three toes and sharp claws was probably made by a Theropod. They were all carnivores.

A footprint with three toes, but the toes are rounded was most likely made by an Ornithopod dinosaur. They were all herbivores.

When there are pairs of prints together that aren't the same size, it was a Sauropod who walked by that day long ago. Their front feet were smaller than their back feet.

If you have several footprints, called a trackway, you can learn even more. You can know if they walked or ran, and how fast they were going.

Could a real dinosaur be born today?

It's fun to think about getting to meet a real dinosaur and what they might be like. There are movies that tell this story. You've probably seen the one called Jurassic Park.

Movie dinos, and other stories about them are science fiction. This means a made-up story with some science in it. In the Jurassic Park movies, a family gets to go to a park where scientists have been able to create real dinosaurs. It makes a great story but isn't real. It isn't possible to create a dinosaur in a lab, and probably never will be. Dinosaur movies have mostly made-up science, not real science.

Scientists might find a way, some day, to create a new dinosaur. They might do it by turning chickens back into their ancient ancestors. But even if they can do this, would it be a good idea? Should there be dinosaurs made by scientists in our world? What do you think?

Did any dinosaurs live underground?

For most of their history, most dinosaurs were too large to live in underground dens. But there might have been some small dinosaurs who did use burrows just like the small mammals did, to find a shelter where the bigger reptiles including dinosaurs couldn't get them!

Oryctodromeus [Orik-tow-drom-ee-us], first discovered in Montana in 2005, was small. It had a snout that could have dug a burrow and the muscles to make digging something it could do. This herbivore lived 95 million years ago. It might have lived in burrows, but there is no proof yet that it, or any other dinosaur, ever did.

Did all dinosaurs lay eggs?

Almost all reptiles, including birds, lay eggs. They don't have live babies. Dinosaurs also built nests and laid eggs, though we aren't sure how the large dinosaurs managed to do this because if they were standing up when they laid their eggs, wouldn't the eggs have broken when they landed in the nest?

Marjungasaurus [Mar-jun-gah-sore-us] has trapped a little Monoophosaurus [Mon-new-foe-sore-us] on a cliff. Using a trap was a smart way to catch an animal that could run faster.

That's a question scientists can't answer yet.

Dinosaur nests and eggs were all sizes and shapes. Eggs could be oblongs, like today's birds' eggs, or shaped like an American football. The largest were as big as a beach ball. Like the reptile eggs of today, dinosaur eggs might have had a hard shell or a soft, leathery shell.

Dinosaur mothers probably had to guard their eggs and protect them from being eaten by predators for a long time, maybe as long as 6 months. Once they hatched, babies had to grow quickly. Paleontologists say that dinosaur hatchlings probably doubled in size in their first six weeks. That's very fast. It takes a human baby about 6 months to double in size after it is born.

Mother dinosaurs might have helped their babies hatch by picking up each egg and gently cracking it open with their teeth. That's what modern crocodiles and alligators do.

What ways did dinosaurs have to defend themselves?

Dinosaurs developed many ways to defend themselves and their eggs or babies. Some could run fast. A few could glide, or fly. The larger, slower dinos developed horns, bony plates like armour and sharp spikes, claws and sharp teeth.

Some could clobber their enemies with their heads and strong necks or wallop them with their long and powerful tails.

Others chose to live in herds for protection, just as herbivores do today.

Dinosaur Fun Fact:

A cheetah can run 130 kilometres per hour, or 81 miles per hour. The fastest runner among dinosaurs we know about was Dromiceiomimus [Drom-i-cee-ee-oh-my-muss]. It lived in the late Cretaceous period and could run up to 60 kilometres per hour, or 37 miles per hour.

Did dinosaurs make any sounds?

It's fun to think about giant animals who go around roaring all the time. But is this what dinosaurs really did?

Modern animals that roar hardly ever do it unless they have to scare away an enemy or claim their own territory. There aren't many modern animals that can roar at all, even if they're big. Whales, the largest animals alive today, don't roar. They click or moan. Other modern animals sing, chirp, whistle, thump, rustle, crow, bark, oink, neigh, cough, growl and make lots of other sounds, but roaring is rare. It makes sense that dinosaurs of all sizes made some kinds of sounds, maybe including some roaring.

But what did they really sound like? Some had strange long tubes attached to their heads that might have been there so they could make some kind of loud sounds, but we don't know what sounds they made. Something like elephants trumpeting, maybe? Or possibly like whales spewing water from their blowholes? Or...what? What dinosaurs sounded like is just another of those intriguing mysteries about dinosaurs that, someday, we might have answers for.

What could dinosaurs hear?

Modern reptiles like alligators, chickens and barn owls have good hearing even though their ears work differently than mammals' ears do. It could be that this reptile way of hearing developed in the common ancestor of alligators, birds and dinosaurs. If so, studying modern reptiles can help us understand how dinosaur hearing worked.

Here's how modern reptile hearing works. They hear a sound with one ear, then hear it separately and a fraction of a second later with the other ear. This very small time difference helps their brain make a map to figure out where the sound is coming from.

Scientists say the time difference is what reptiles use to create a map in their brain and that this way of hearing evolved before the Age of Dinosaurs.

Tyrannosaurus rex

Lived 68 million years ago to 65.5 million years ago

Tyrannosaurus rex [Tie-ran-oh-sore-us wrecks] was a big bruiser of a dinosaur that walked on its back legs, had small arms and a huge head with powerful jaws. It could be 6 metres, or almost 20 feet tall.

Its teeth were 12 inches, or 30.5 centimetres long. Its bite force was three times as much as a modern shark.

Large members of the Tyrannosaurus family like Tyrannosaurus rex and Daspletosaurus [Dass-plet-oh-sore-us] crunched up and swallowed the bones of their victims.

The huge nostrils in its skull mean this dinosaur probably had excellent smelling abilities.

Dinosaur Fun Fact:
A T-rex skull is so big you could easily fit inside it.

Tyrannosaurus rex battling a snake. Snakes evolved during the Cretaceous Era.

T-rex was a skilled hunter that preyed on other dinosaurs. Their fossils have been found in Western United States and in Western China.

It was a large and heavy animal, so it might not have been able to run very fast, or at all.

Their short arms might look wimpy, but Tyrannosaurus rex had claws on its hands that could slash and seriously wound other dinosaurs. Their claws were a metre, or 3 feet long and sharp.

The enemies of Tyrannosaurus rex that could injure or kill it include other big dinosaurs like Spinosaurus and Triceratops. There were also illnesses all types of dinosaurs could get that could kill them, like avian flu and cancer. And many dinosaurs probably died when their battle wounds got infected or broken bones meant they could no longer hunt or find water.

Dilong

Lived 128 million years ago

Dilong [Dee-long], found in Asia, was a small, early tyrannosaur that lived 60 million years before T-rex. It weighed just 25 pounds, or 11 kilograms.

This little guy was covered in feathers, though it couldn't fly.

Dinosaur Fun Fact:

Dinosaur bones have growth rings on them, just like trees do. By counting the rings, you can know how old the dinosaur was when it died.

What happened when?

BILLIONS of years ago:

4.6   Our solar system is formed.

3.7   The first one-cell animals appear.

MILLIONS of years ago:

530   The first fish appear in the ocean.

500   The first plants grow on land.

480   The first insects appear.

450   The first sharks evolve in the ocean.

385   Some fish leave the water to become amphibians.

330   Some amphibians evolve into the first reptiles.

230   **A new kind of reptile is born – the dinosaurs.**

175	Supercontinent Pangea splits into two continents.
130	The first flowers appear on trees and plants.
65.5	**The K-T Extinction ends the Age of Dinosaurs.**
2	The first humans appear in Africa.

THOUSANDS of years ago:

300	Modern humans evolve in Africa.

Dinosaur Fun Fact:
The most complete Tyrannosaurus rex fossil skeleton was found in South Dakota, U.S., in 1990. Paleontologists found about 90 % of her and named her Sue. She got her name from Sue Hendrickson, an explorer and fossil collector who found her in 1990. You can visit Sue the T-rex at the Field Museum of Natural History in Chicago.

Pachyrhinosaurus was a herbivore that lived in herds in North America.

Pachyrhinosaurus

Lived 74 to 65.5 million years ago

Pachyrhinosaurus [Pack-ee-rye-know-sore-us] lived in Western Canada and Alaska.

When they were adults they were 6 to 8 metres or about 20 to 26 feet long. They could weigh 3 to almost 4 tonnes or 3.3 to 4.0 tons.

Heavy bony body armour helped protect Pachyrhinosaurus from the carnivore dinosaurs like T-rex.

Albertosaurus

Lived 73 million years ago to 69 million years ago

[Al-bert-oh-sore-us] was 8 to 10 metres or 26 to 33 feet long. That's as long as a school bus. It was in the Tyannosaur family of dinosaurs and was found in Alberta, Canada.

It became extinct about a million years before Tyrannosaurus rex appeared on Earth.

Albertosaurus was the first meat-eating dinosaur ever discovered in Canada. It had scales and small horns in front of each eye.

Triceratops

Lived 68 to 66 million years ago

Triceratops [Try-sare-a-tops] had hundreds of teeth and a parrot-like beak. It was a plant-eater.

It had three horns. Two of these were large horns on top of its head. Their third horn was above their snout. They also had a large bony frill that worked like a shield.

We know very little about most of the types of dinosaurs already discovered because only one or only a few of their kind have been found.

That's not true for Triceratops. Of every 10 dinosaur fossils found in the Hell Creek Formation in Western United States, four of them are Triceratops.

This is Triceratops. Their huge head was one-third of the total length of their body.

The horn on Triceratops' nose was made out of keratin, like human fingernails. This horn wouldn't have helped this animal very much in a fight. Scientists aren't sure what their nose horn was for or how it worked. Maybe it was just there to help them attract their mates. Or possibly their nose horn made a sound, something like having a nose trumpet.

Velociraptor

Lived: 75 million to 71 million years ago

Velociraptor [Vell-oh-seer-rap-tor] is a dinosaur you might have seen at the movies. Or maybe not! There was a Velociraptor in Jurassic Park, but that dino movie star was really a lot more like a different real

Velociraptor was a bird-like dinosaur and a stealth hunter.

dinosaur, the Utahraptor, than it was like the real Velociraptor.

Velociraptor was a smaller dinosaur, at only about two feet, or 61 centimetres tall. That's about as tall as a modern turkey, but it was a lot longer than a turkey at 6 feet, or 1.8 metres long. It had strong back legs, allowing it to run about 24 miles per hour, or 39 kilometres per hour. Though it could probably run faster than most of the mammals, small lizards and baby dinos it ate, maybe it didn't have to run very often.

The reason is that Velociraptor was a stealth hunter, like modern tigers. It would hide and watch, waiting for the right moment to leap out at an unsuspecting creature, stand on one back leg, and use a deadly curved claw on the other foot to slash its victim. Then it would wait for the wounded animal to bleed to death.

Velociraptor had two of these claw weapons, one on the second toe of each back foot.

It had hollow bones and feathers like modern birds but couldn't fly. This dino lived only in Central and Eastern Asia.

Velociraptor had a larger brain than modern birds, compared to the size of its body, but probably wasn't much smarter than the average modern bird. It had an excellent sense of smell, probably to help with hunting and ambushing its prey. It killed them with its hooked claws and ate them with its 60 teeth. It probably also robbed other dino nests. It could easily stand on one leg, using its tail for balance. It lived in Mongolia and China.

Stegosaurus

Lived 155 million years ago to 150 million years ago

Stegosaurus [Stay-goh-sore-us] had massive plates sticking up from its spine. These might have been to help it warm up in the sun, or help it cool off when it was too hot out. Each one of these back plates were 30 inches, or 76 centimetres long. These plates are called "scutes."

Though it was a large animal, its brain was only about as big as a walnut.

A Brachiosaurus [Brak-ee-uh-sore-us], on the left, and a Stegosaurus face off at a watering hole.

Brachiosaurus

Lived 161.2 million years ago to 145 million years ago

Brachiosaurus was a massive long-neck that lived all over the world. Like Diplodocus, it stood on its strong back legs to browse from trees.

As a typical Sauropod, it had a long neck filled with air sacks and only a very small heart for the size of its body.

Brachiosaurus was 69 feet, or about 21 metres long when it was an adult. That's about as long as two school buses.

To defend itself, it might have used its very long neck and head like a club, the way fighting giraffes do today.

This dinosaur is Spinosaurus. With a crocodile-like face, it was very good at catching fish. It caught and ate sawfish, lungfish and sharks.

Spinosaurus

Lived 112 million years ago to 93.5 million years ago

Spinosaurus [Spine-oh-sore-us] was 52 to 59 feet long or 16 to 18 metres long. Adults weighted three times as much as T-rex, or about 20 tonnes or 22 tons.

This dinosaur used its long crocodile-like snout for catching fish. It could also hunt on land.

Spinosaurus was larger than Giganotosaurus and Tyrannosaurus rex.

Spinosaurus could swim, using its tail like fish do to motor through the water.

Giganotosaurus was a Theropod dinosaur that lived in Argentina. Theropods walked on their two back legs. Each foot had three toes.

Giganotosaurus

Lived 99.6 million years ago to 93.5 million years ago

Giganotosaurus [Ge-eye-gan-oh-toe-sore-us] is another enormous meat-eater that killed its food but was also a scavenger. It lived in Argentina. It had sharp but thin teeth, like shark teeth. It would slice its prey until that animal bled to death while the Giganotosaurus waited for its feast.

Dinosaur Fun Fact:

When dinosaurs lived there, Antarctica was tropical, about as warm and humid as Florida is in summer.

Diplodocus

Lived 154 million years ago to 152 million years ago

Diplodocus [Dip-low-dock-us] was a Sauropod discovered in Western United States. It walked on all four feet. Its hind legs were longer than the front legs, so this animal's body sloped downwards from the hips to the shoulders.

It was able to stand up on its hind legs, leaning back on its powerful tail so it could reach the more tender leaves higher up in trees.

Diplodocus had the longest tail of any animal that has ever lived. In adults, its tail could be up to 46 feet, or 14 metres long. It had pencil-shaped teeth that it used to strip leaves off branches. It couldn't chew these leaves, so it swallowed them whole.

Europasaurus

Lived in the late Jurassic Period

Not all the Sauropods were slow-moving leaf eaters and as big as a barn. Europasaurus [Your-oh-pa-sore-us] was only as big as a modern bison. Adults weren't any larger than about 10 feet or 3 metres long. They probably weighed less than 2,000 pounds or 900 kilograms.

Here's why this Sauropod was so small, compared to its Diplodocus and Brachiosaurus cousins. It lived on a small island, totally cut off from the mainland. Islands give animals a smaller territory. They may need to be smaller, and so eat less food, to survive. It's common on islands for animals to evolve to look different, and usually smaller, than their mainland ancestors.

Magyarosaurus

Lived 83.5 million years ago to 65.5 million years ago

Magyarosaurus [Mag-yar-oh-sore-us] was a Titanosaur. Titanosaurs were the Sauropods with body armour. Magyarosaurus weighed only about .9 tonne or one ton. Other Titanosaurs, like Argentinosaurus, could weigh 100 times as much as Magyarosaurus!

Some paleontologists think that this Titanosaur liked to eat underwater plants. It did this by sticking its head underwater and grazing on the seaweed and other plants that grew in shallow water. That's the same underwater grazing method modern ducks use.

Camarasaurus

Lived 155 million years ago to 145 million years ago

Diplodocus and Apatosaurus get lots of attention in the dino world, but the most common Sauropod in the late Jurassic Period in North America was Camarasaurus [Ca-mar-ruh-sore-us]. This long-necked plant-eater only weighed about 20 tons or 18 tonnes. That's about as heavy as three adult African elephants. That's also about half as big as the biggest Sauropods.

Many Camarasaurus fossils have been found in Western United States and Mexico. There are usually

Camarasaurus was about as tall as a modern giraffe.

many animals grouped together. This is why paleontologists think that there were vast herds of Camarasaurus about 150 million years ago. They ate fern leaves and conifers. Adults were 15 feet or 5 metres tall, about the same as a modern female giraffe. They were 59 feet, or 18 metres long from head to tail.

Brontosaurus

Lived 156 to 146 million years ago

Brontosaurus [Brawn-toe-sore-us] is another big Sauropod. It could grow to be 72 feet or 22 metres long. It might have been able to crack its long tail like a whip. If so, that would have been a terrifying weapon!

It could weight up to 34.5 tonnes, or 38 tons.

Like some modern birds, Brontosaurus ate stones to help grind up and digest the plants and leaves it ate.

Argentinosaurus

Lived 97 million years ago to 93.5 million years ago

Argentinosaurus [Ar-gen-tin-oh-sore-us] was a Sauropod that lived in Argentina, South America. Like other Sauropods, the way it digested food was to ferment it in their stomachs. This means it would have been smelly to live with them, because Sauropods would have farted almost all the time.

This large dinosaur could be 115 feet or 35 metres long. That's about as long as four fire engines. It was 24 feet or 7.3 metres tall at the shoulder. It was also a heavy animal, weighing about 90 tonnes, or 99 tons as an adult. That's 198,417 pounds or 90,000 kilograms!

Their food for just one day would make a leaf pile as big as a bus! A herd of these animals wouldn't take long to eat an entire forest! For this reason, they would need to move around their territory, giving the trees a chance to grow back again.

Argentinosaurus probably had to be eating almost all the time when it was awake to fuel its huge body!

Microraptor

Lived 120 million years ago

Some small Theropod dinosaurs evolved into birds during the late Jurassic and Cretaceous periods. One of these was Microraptor [My-crow-rap-tore], a small, feathered creature with four wings. It could glide but might not have been able to fly.

This dino-bird had four wings and a feathered tail. If it was a glider, it would climb trees, then glide between them until it got down to the ground again. Being light enough and strong enough to flap its wings and fly would be a big advantage to such a small creature. That kind of advantage probably took thousands or maybe millions of years to evolve.

Microraptors were among the first feathered dinosaurs to be discovered. More than 300 fossil Microraptors have been found. Scientists think that the largest Microraptor wouldn't have been any bigger than 1.2 meters or almost 4 feet long.

Unlike any other kind of dinosaur Microraptor only ate insects.

Dinosaur Fun Fact:
How long did dinosaurs live for? Where they like modern animals that usually don't live more than 20 or 30 years? It's hard to know, though some paleontologists suspect that some dinosaurs could live for much longer, perhaps as long as 200 years or more.

Microraptor might have been as colorful as modern tropical birds.

A Baryonyx hunting for a meal.

Baryonyx

Lived Early Cretaceous Era

Baryonyx [Barry-on-icks] was a strange dinosaur, sort of a mix between a dinosaur and a crocodile, with very long jaws and straight pointed teeth that were cone-shaped. One was found with fish scales and part of an Iguanodon in its stomach.

It was 10 metres or 33 feet long and lived in England and Spain.

Dinosaur Fun Fact:

The very first dragon teeth fossils were found in China 3,500 years ago. People didn't know what they were but thought they must be dragon teeth. Strangely, dragons in movies look very much like some dinosaurs.

Allosaurus was a Theropod with claws the shape and size of a ripe banana.

Allosaurus

Lived 154 to 145 million years ago

Allosaurus [All-oh-sore-us] lived in North America, Europe and possibly Africa. Its fossils have been discovered in Colorado, Utah and Wyoming in United States and also in Portugal.

It had a pair of horns above and in front of its eyes, but scientists don't know why. The horns were too small to be useful in fighting. Maybe they were just there to impress other Allosauruses.

Allosaurus was the top predator. It could use its head like an axe to hack into prey like Camptosaurus, Brontosaurus and Stegosaurus. This is the dinosaur

This is what a living Ceratosaurus may have looked like.

that paleontologists call "The Butcher" for its fiercely sharp teeth and claws.

Ceratosaurus

Lived 153 million years ago to 148 million years ago

Ceratosaurus [Sera-toe-sore-us] had a horn on its nose and big ridges over the eyes. This medium-sized Theropod was found as a nearly complete fossil skeleton in Colorado, United States. Ceratosaurus is a close cousin of two dinosaurs first found in South America. They are Abelisaurus and Carnotaurus.

Fossil footprints of Ceratosaurus show that this meat-eater probably hunted in packs. It ate plant-eating dinosaurs. Some scientists believe this dinosaur also caught and ate fish, turtles and crocodiles.

Dilophosaurus

Lived: 190 million to 200 million years ago until about 175 million years ago

In the movie Jurassic Park, Dilophosaurus [Dill-off-oh-sore-us] was a cute dog-sized dinosaur with a big neck frill that could spit poison. None of this was true. The real Dilophosaurus was much larger, had no frill and didn't spit poison. No dinosaur ever found had poison spit.

Their name means "two-crested lizard" and that's the first strange and true fact about Dilophosaurus. They did have two crests on their heads. These crests weren't strong enough for fighting, so what were they for? It might have been to attract a mate, just like modern male songbirds use their bright feather colors. Or possibly these dinos could recognize each other by their own unique head crests.

Dilophosaurus adults could grow to be 23 feet, or about 7 metres long and weigh 1,000 pounds, or 454 kilograms. That was very large, for their time. They lived in the early Jurassic period. Their bones, fossils and footprints have been found in United States and China. There were Dilophosauruses for about 20 million years. Then they vanished. No one knows why, but they were gone long before the extinction event that ended the time of dinosaurs on Earth.

This is Minmi, named for where they were found in Australia.

Dilophosaurus walked on two legs. They could use their hands to hold objects. They had large claws, but probably weren't good fighters. They probably were scavengers. Or they caught fish. Their body shape shows that they were probably good swimmers.

Their lower teeth were much smaller than their upper teeth. Though their teeth were shaped like a modern crocodile's teeth, they didn't have nearly as much bite strength.

In the United States, the first evidence of this dinosaur was found on Navajo Nation land in Arizona. Later, tracks were found in Connecticut, leading to Dilophosaurus being named the official State Dinosaur in Connecticut. You can see Dilophosaurus tracks at Dinosaur State Park in Connecticut.

Minmi

Lived in the Early Cretaceous

Minmi [Min-mee] is the dinosaur with the shortest name. It didn't get this name because it was a mini-me, but because it was found near Minmi Crossing in Queensland, Australia.

Minmi had long legs so probably it could run fast. The spines on its hips helped it defend itself.

An early Ankylosaur, Minmi adults weighed about 500 pounds, or 27 kilograms. That's much smaller than its cousins, the massive Ankylosaurs of the later Cretaceous like Ankylosaurus and Euoplocephalus.

Suzhousaurus

Lived 145 million years ago to 100 years ago

Suzhousaurus [Sooze-ho-soar-us] looked like a mash-up between a giant rat and a giant sloth. It had a furry body, walked upright and could be 3 metres, or almost 10 feet tall and weigh 1,300 kilograms, or 2,860 pounds!

This Theropod had a pot-belly, giant claws, a body covered in feathers, a head like a turkey and huge arms. It's the only dinosaur we know of that waddled.

It was found in the Ganzu province of China.

Cryolophosaurus was a fast runner, reaching a top speed of about 40 miles per hour, or 64 kilometres per hour.

Cryolophosaurus

Lived: Early Jurassic period, 170 million years ago

Cryolophosaurus [cry-oh-loff-o-sore-us] looked something like Tyrannosaurus rex, but they were not related to each other. Cryolophosaurus were meat-eaters. They had horns coming up from their eye sockets and a stiff crest shaped like a fan on their heads. For their crest shape, some experts call this dinosaur "Elvisaurus."

Pegomastax

Lived in the early Jurassic Era

Pegomastax [Peggo-mast-ax] was a plant-eater that had a beak and teeth. It had a parrot face, but a porcupine body, covered in quills. This little dino was

Gigantoraptor had a beak but no teeth and was probably a plant-eater. Its large, strong back legs meant it would have been a good runner, like a modern ostrich.

just 2 feet, or about 60 centimetres, long. Only one has ever been found, in South Africa.

Gigantoraptor

Lived 71 million years ago to 65 million years ago

Gigantoraptor [Gi-gan-tor-rap-tor] had a face and feathers like a chicken. A really big chicken. It could grow to be 5 metres, or almost 16.5 feet tall and weight up to 2,000 kilograms, or 4,400 pounds.

Dinosaur Fun Fact:

Why did some dinosaurs need such long tails? It was because their tail gave them balance so they could lean forward to run.

An artist's idea of what it would have looked like if Dakotaraptor, on the right, attacked a Mamenchisaurus. This couldn't actually have happened, because these animals didn't live in the same time period.

Mamenchisaurus

Lived 163.5 million years ago to 139.8 million years ago

Mamenchisaurus [Ma-men-chee-sore-us] was a long-neck with a spectacularly long neck, the longest of any dinosaur ever found. This animal lived in China and was 26 metres or 85 feet long. Half of that length was their neck! It weighed about 16 tonnes or 18 tons.

An adult Mamenchisaurus would need to eat 1,150 pounds or 525 kilograms of leaves every day to survive.

Dakotaraptor

Lived 70.6 million years ago to 65.5 million years ago

Dakotaraptor [Da-coat-ta-rap-tor] was 4.35 to 6 metres or 14.3 to 19.7 feet long. An adult weighed 220 to 350 kilograms or 485 to 772 pounds. It was found in South Dakota, United States and is a close cousin of Utahraptor.

Jeholopterus

Lived 164.7 million years ago to 161.2 million years ago

Jeholopterus [Je-hoe-lop-ter-us] is called the vampire dinosaur because it was a blood-sucker. It looked like a bat with a lot of sharp teeth and could glide, but it probably couldn't fly. It lived by attaching itself to the bellies of bigger dinosaurs, where it sucked their blood.

Incisivorsaurus

Lived 125 million years ago to 122.46 million years ago

Incisivorsaurus [In-sis-i-vor-sore-us] had teeth like a rat, a raptor face, an ostrich body with feathers and big chicken feet. Its front arms looked just like wings, but it couldn't fly. It was a smaller dino, just 1 metre or 3 feet tall or long. It weighed about 6 kilograms, or about 13 pounds.

In a short race, Gallimimus could run faster than a racehorse can today.

Gallimimus

Lived 70 million years ago

Gallimimus [Gal-ih-my-mus] is an Ornithomimosaur [Or-nith-hoe-my-moe-sore], a group also called the ostrich dinosaurs because they're a lot like modern ostriches.

Like an ostrich, this dinosaur had a long neck and long, powerful legs that allowed them to be strong and fast runners.

They had feathers and beaks but no teeth.

Gallimimus lived in Mongolia, Asia.

Hypsilophodon

Lived 130 million years ago to 125 million years ago

Hypsilophodon [Hips-ill-oh-foe-don] had long legs, a stiff tail and a beak with teeth. It was found in England and might have been an omnivore.

When it was first discovered, scientists thought it might have been a tree-climbing, kangaroo type of animal. Now we know that couldn't be true. Hypsilophodon adults could grow to be 1.8 metres or almost 6 feet long and weigh about 20 kilograms or 45 pounds. They were good runners.

Pantydraco

Lived in the late Triassic Era

Pantydraco [Pan-tee-drak-co] was small, just 3 metres or 10 feet long. Only one Pantydraco fossil has ever been found in Wales.

This dinosaur might have the funniest name of any animal. But their name doesn't mean underwear. It comes from a Welsh word that means a well or spring, plus draco, which means dragon.

Dinosaur Fun Fact:

All the carnivore, or meat-eating, dinosaurs walked on their two back feet and used their front feet as hands. All the plant-eaters, or herbivores, walked on all four feet, though some could stand on their back legs to reach food.

A Deinonychus searching for a meal.

Deinonychus

Lived 115 million years ago to 108 million years ago

Deinonychus [Deen-oh-nie-chuss] was a smaller dinosaur, just 4 metres or 13 feet long.

Deinonychus liked to live in swamps. Its long claws could be 5 inches, or almost 13 centimetres long.

A carnivore, it probably hunted smaller reptiles and mammals. It might have hunted in packs and, if so, it could have gone after larger animals.

Dinosaur Fun Fact:
Dinosaurs swallowed rocks to help grind up and digest their food. Birds swallow small stones for the same reason today.

Carnotaurus had scales, but no feathers. It was found in South America.

Carnotaurus

Lived 83.5 million years ago to 65.5 million years ago

Carnotaurus [Carn-oh-tar-us] was a Theropod and had the smallest arms of any dinosaur. Their arms were only ¼ as long as their heads. It was a strong and fast runner and is also a movie star because Carnotaurus was in the Disney animated movie Dinosaur. Unfortunately, in the movie it looked more like Tyrannosaurus Rex. The real Carnotaurus had flat-topped horns that might have been for head-butting competitions with other Carnotauruses, something like the way modern male deer fight today.

Dinosaur Fun Fact:
Dinosaurs had bones that are almost hollow, just like modern birds.

Parasaurolophus was a Hadrosaur. Hadrosaurs were duck-billed dinosaurs. The little animal on the left is a mammal.

Parasaurolophus

Lived 76.5 million years ago to 73 million years ago

Parasaurolophus [Pair-a-sore-oh-lop-us] had a crest with tubes on the back of its scull. Scientists believe these tubes were for making loud trumpeting sounds. If so, these sounds could probably have been heard for great distances. The sounds might have been used in the same way bird's calls and songs are today. That is, to defend a territory or find a mate.

The tubes in the crest went from their nostrils, or nose opening to the back of the crest and then back towards their head.

A Troodon mother defends her nest in this museum exhibit.

Troodon

Lived in the late Cretaceous Era

Troodon [True-don] might have been the smartest dinosaur that ever lived, many paleontologists say. Even so, it was probably only about as smart as a modern racoon or beaver.

It had teeth with a serrated edge, like a steak knife. It also had a curved killing claw on each foot.

It was 2 metres, or 6 feet long. Its large eyes gave it good night vision, so that's probably when it hunted. It could grab and hold onto things with its three-fingered hands. It ate smaller mammals, fish, birds, snakes or the eggs of other dinosaurs.

Ankylosaurus was a herbivore that lived in what is now Montana, United States.

Ankylosaurus

Lived 68 million years ago to 66 million years ago

Ankylosaurus [Ank-kill-low-sore-us] had bony plate armour and looked like a tubby lizard tank with a club at the end of its tail. It was 10 metres or 33 feet long.

Their bony plate armour was almost impossible for their enemies to bite through. Ankylosaurus would turn its back on an enemy, like Tyrannosaurus rex, any time they met up. That's because Ankylosaurus walked on all-fours, but it had a powerful tail shaped like a club. If the T-rex got close enough, Ankylosaurus could smash its enemy's ankles, bringing down its giant rival.

Coelophysis was a fast runner with sharp, jagged teeth. They hunted in packs.

Coelophysis

Lived 225 million to 190 million years ago

Coelophysis [See-low-fie-sis] is a dinosaur that scientists know more about than most of the others discovered so far. That's because the fossil bones of thousands of Coelophysises have been found in Arizona and New Mexico in United States and also in southern Africa.

Adults were only a metre or 3 feet high and 3 metres or 9 feet long. They weighed about 100 pounds, or 45 kilograms. They hunted and ate other reptiles, mammals, and birds. One was found with the bones of a small crocodile in its belly.

This is the first dinosaur that we know of to have a furcula bone. All modern birds have a furcula bone. You probably know this bone because it's also called a wishbone. Without it, birds can't fly. Coelophysis couldn't fly, either. Scientists are still puzzled about why it had a wishbone.

Plateosaurus

Lived 214 million years ago to 204 million years ago

Plateosaurus [Plat-ee-oh-sore-us] was a long-neck with small, leaf-shaped teeth. It lived in Greenland and Northern Europe. An adult Plateosaurus was 5 to 10 metres or 16 to 33 feet long. It was a prey animal and a herd animal.

So far, paleontologists have found more than 100 Plateosaurus fossils.

Ozraptor

Lived 170 million years ago

Ozraptor [Ahhs-rap-tor] was a Theropod that lived in Australia. Only one part of a leg bone of one animal has ever been found. That was by some schoolboys, back in 1966.

It was probably about 3 metres, or 10 feet tall. Until another Ozraptor is found, that might be all scientists can know about this animal.

A pair of Iguanodons by the coast.

Iguanodon

Lived 126 million years ago to 113 million years ago

Iguanodon [Eee-gwan-oh-don] lived in what is now England, Spain and Belgium in Europe. It was one of the first three dinosaurs to be discovered and named and was an herbivore.

Iguanodon was 10 metres, or almost 33 feet long. It had very odd hands on its arms. Each hand had a thumb spike, three fingers that were like hooves and a long fifth finger that could hold things.

Dinosaur Fun Fact:
Most dinosaurs had feathers but didn't have scales. All of the reptiles alive today have scales. Only the birds have feathers.

Rajasaurus, a Theropod like all the Tyrannosaurs, lived in India in the late Cretaceous Era. At that time, India was an island with many active volcanos. Later, India would drift north and become part of Asia.

The day the dinosaurs died

We don't know if it was a hot summer day, or a breezy day in Autumn. We also don't know what time this happened. It might have been during the day. Or at night. We don't even know what year this happened.

Until just 42 years ago, scientists weren't even sure this DID happen. That's when they finally found proof that one day 65.5 million years ago was the last day of the great Age of Dinosaurs. On that day, hundreds of thousands of dinosaurs died.

Scientists had long suspected that something very bad had happened to wipe out all the dinosaurs. They just weren't sure what.

The answer came from outer space. On a warm, lush day like any other in the tropical Cretaceous Era, an asteroid going 30 kilometres per second or 67,108 miles per hour slammed into Earth. It happened just off the Yucatan Penninsula in Mexico.

Scientists now know this happened because the asteroid, or it might have been a comet, brought iridium with it and buried it in the ocean. Iridium is a metal that is rare near Earth's surface but common, meaning there's lots of it, in space rocks like asteroids. For there to be a layer of iridium buried off Yucatan there had to be an asteroid hit. The crater it left was also proof.

When this asteroid hit, everything nearby was immediately vapourized. The impact sent shock waves through the centre of earth. It caused tsunamis and volcanoes to erupt. The skies darkened and rained super-heated stones that caused forest fires.

Not all the dinosaurs died right away. Some found shelter, though because they were so large, few were as lucky as the smaller creatures like mammals, snakes, insects and birds. Most of them found hiding places underground. Fish and ocean creatures that could swim deeper also survived.

As the smoke blocked out the sun, plants began to die. The animals that ate the plants also died. At first, the meat-eating dinosaurs that were still alive would have had plenty of dead herbivores to eat. Soon, that

Torosaurus [Tor-oh-sore-us] was an herbivore that lived in Western Canada and Western United States at the end of the Mesozoic Era. This is one of the kinds of dinosaurs that died out in the K-T Extinction that ended the Age of Dinosaurs.

was no longer true. It must have been terrifying for them.

It could be that some – maybe only a few -- dinosaurs were able to survive if they lived very far away from where the asteroid hit earth. There were many small animals that did survive, perhaps by hibernating, or eating roots or insects or fish. Dinosaurs, with their big bodies, needed a lot of food. There simply wasn't enough left for them to eat after the K-T Extinction. That's what scientists call this asteroid disaster that ended the Age of Dinosaurs.

The K-T Extinction was a Mass Extinction Event. That's a change on Earth that is so huge and so sudden that plants and animals have no time to adjust to the change. They don't get the time to evolve to cope with these big changes. Many of them, or most of them, become extinct.

There have been seven mass extinction events in all of Earth's history. All these mass extinction events happened very long ago. In each one, the climate changed. Suddenly, some animals could no longer exist. Others that could live in the new conditions on Earth would soon take their place.

We don't know if the world stayed dark for weeks, or months, or even years after the asteroid hit Earth. We do know that 75 percent of all the animals alive before the asteroid hit earth died on that day or not long after. Yet, somehow, many plants and animals did survive. Ferns, evergreen trees and grasses lived. So did birds, insects, many types of reptiles including crocodiles, amphibians and small mammals. Sharks, jellyfish, frogs, scorpions, fish, snakes and turtles all

Eohippus [EEE-oh-hip-us] was a small mammal that survived the K-T Extinction. It later evolved into horses.

survived. They are all the ancestors of all the plants and animals on Earth today.

What the dinosaurs left behind for us to find is more than just a few bones, some fossils and footprints. They left us to marvel at their size, their diversity, their oddness, and most of all their longevity. That means how long they survived. They dominated Earth for millions of years. They learned how to adapt and change when they had to.

Dinosaurs are the most successful animal that has ever lived.

Today, they inspire us, in art and stories, in movies and even in cartoons and colouring books. They also

A bald eagle sits on the skull of Tyrannosaurus rex, its ancient distant cousin.

remind us that life on Earth is always changing and evolving.

After the dinosaurs died

The K-T Extinction ended the Age of Dinosaurs and also the Age of Reptiles. The next age, called the Paleogene [Pay-lee-oh-jean] Era, 65 million years ago to 23 million years ago, would become the Age of Mammals. In this time, true horses, rodents, rhinoceros and elephants would evolve. By the end of the Paleogene Era there were also dogs, pigs and cats.

What have humans learnt from dinosaurs?

Dinosaurs lived for more than 165 million years. They were the dominant animals everywhere on Earth from the middle of the Triassic Era to the end of the Cretaceous Era. That made them masters of the planet for more than 65 million years. Because there are none now, we think of them as an animal that was not successful, a failed animal. This isn't true. Dinosaurs were very successful, for a very long time. They were strange and magnificent animals. Some of them were the largest vertebrate animals that have ever lived. Vertebrate animal means animal with a backbone.

"It is not the strongest of the species that survives, nor the most intelligent that survives. It is the one that is the most adaptable to change." - Charles Darwin

This book is not long enough to talk about ALL the dinosaurs. There are always more dinos to find and more to discover about their mysterious, ancient past lives.

Dinosaurs were a lot like us. They had full lives. They ate, slept, fought, and probably, like all animals, they played. They grew up and had their families. Some of them grew old. They lived their lives every day, just as modern animals do.

Their end time came. This is true for all types of animals. When they go, someone else always takes their place. This was true in their time and is true now.

Some paleontologists believe that when the K-T Extinction Event happened, dinosaurs were already in decline. Their best days had come and gone and their Glory Days were over. That might be true. Even so, it's thrilling to wonder about them and their real lives and imagine what it must have been like, when the dinosaurs ruled Earth!

Thanks for reading!

Jacquelyn

Dinosaur Fun Fact:
Though dinosaurs did not survive very long after the K-T Extinction, many animals did. There have been seven major, and many more minor, extinction events that changed animal history. Only one group of animals has survived every one of these extinction events. That group is the amphibians.

Dinosaur Fun Fact:
There is an animal alive today that is larger than any dinosaur every discovered. That animal is the Blue Whale. It can reach 108 feet, or 33 metres long. The first whales evolved on Earth about 50 million years ago. Whales and dolphins have bigger brains than any of the dinosaurs had.

About the Author

Jacquelyn Elnor Johnson started telling stories to entertain her younger sisters when she was 10. They were a tough audience! By age 15, she was a writing for the local newspaper and had written her first book. She went on to have careers in writing for and editing newspapers and magazines and teaching journalism in United States and Canada.

In 2014, she moved with her family to Nova Scotia, drawn by the opportunity to live near the ocean. A life-long pet lover, she is the bestselling author of 15 books about caring for and enjoying pets and animals, including **I Want A Bearded Dragon** and **The Complete Bearded Dragon Care Book**.

She also writes novels including the Morley Stories series for girls ages 10 to 13.

Find all her books and more at **www.CrimsonHillBooks.com**

PHOTO CREDITS

Thank you to lead artist **Daniel Eskridge**, who created all the dinosaurs on the cover and 28 of the illustrations in this book. While no one knows exactly what these amazing animals really looked like, Daniel has used his skills, knowledge and admiration for dinosaurs to draw them in their true surroundings and as accurately as scientists are able to describe them today.

We also are grateful for the works of these artists:

Pixabay: ICor1031, ELG21, Oltre Creative Agency, and Public Domain Pictures.

Shutterstock: Dotted Yeti, Ferhat Cinar of Rodos Studio, Elenarts, Michael Rosskothen, Kostiantyn Ivanyshen, Danny Ye, Natalia Van D, Kamomeen, Andrew M. Allport and Catmando.

Loved all these great dinosaur facts? Discover MORE Fun Facts books from Crimson Hill Books:

- **Fun Dog Facts for Kids**
- **Fun Cat Facts for Kids**
- **Fun Leopard Gecko and Bearded Dragon Facts for Kids**
- **Fun Reptile Facts for Kids; Lizards, Turtles, Crocodilians, Snakes and Birds**
- **Fun Pony Facts for Kids**
- **Fun Horse Facts for Kids**
- **Fun Bird Facts for Kids**
- **Fun Backyard Bird Facts for Kids**
- **Fun Insect Facts for Kids**

And Don't Miss:

- **Dinosaur Facts for Kids**
- **T-rex Facts for Kids**